In three short books, Pastor Joe Thorn offers a helpful treatment on the local church that is biblical, baptistic, and Calvinistic—and simultaneously fresh and practical. This is ideal for those who desire a better understanding of what the church is designed to be and do as a community of faith seeking to follow Jesus into the world with the gospel.

In *The Heart of the Church*, Thorn walks the reader through the gospel and related doctrines, demonstrating how what we believe forms who we are as God's people. In *The Character of the Church*, the essential components of a church are laid out in a clear and practical way, showing what is needed for overall church health. In *The Life of the Church*, Thorn offers a fresh perspective on how the church can live on mission for the glory of God and the good of others in tangible ways.

ED STETZER
Billy Graham Distinguished Chair, Wheaton College

———

I'd like to pass out *The Character of the Church* to every one of our church members. It's that good! It's a simple yet profound primer on the nature of the church. It gives a brief overview on the authority of the Bible, the ordinances, matters of church membership, and church discipline. These are essential for all believers to know and understand.

DAVE FURMAN
Pastor, Redeemer Church of Dubai, and author of *Being There: How to Love Those Who Are Hurting*

The Life of the Church is a helpful treatise on worship that will edify the church. Joe is careful to ensure his exhortations spring from Scripture itself, which makes this book applicable for Christians everywhere. It was a joy to read about the many aspects of the life that Christ has purchased for us with His own blood.

GLORIA FURMAN
Cross-cultural worker and author of *Missional Motherhood* and *Alive in Him*

———

The Heart of the Church is a brief and accessible theology of the gospel. It is simple, but not simplistic. It offers profound truths in everyday language. This book will help new Christians and serve as an encouraging reminder to mature ones.

RICHARD C. BARCELLOS
Pastor, Grace Reformed Baptist Church in Palmdale, CA, and author of *The Lord's Supper as a Means of Grace*

THE

character

OF THE

CHURCH

—

THE MARKS OF GOD'S
OBEDIENT PEOPLE

—

JOE THORN

MOODY PUBLISHERS
CHICAGO

Scripture quotations are from the ESV® Bible (The Holy Bible, English Standard Version®), copyright © 2001 by Crossway, a publishing ministry of Good News Publishers. Used by permission. All rights reserved.

Edited by Kevin P. Emmert
Cover and Interior Design: Erik M. Peterson
Author photo: Anthony Benedetto

ISBN: 978-0-8024-1471-7

We hope you enjoy this book from Moody Publishers. Our goal is to provide high-quality, thought-provoking books and products that connect truth to your real needs and challenges. For more information on other books and products written and produced from a biblical perspective, go to www.moodypublishers.com or write to:

Moody Publishers
820 N. LaSalle Boulevard
Chicago, IL 60610

1 3 5 7 9 10 8 6 4 2

Printed in the United States of America

To the elders of Redeemer Fellowship,
who have been instrumental in forming
the character of the church we serve.

contents

INTRODUCTION

L ocal churches of Jesus Christ are called to be shining lights on hills, illuminating the world with the beauty of truth and godliness. But these lights dim when their character weakens and their focus is lost.

Most Christians understand that a church is not a building. Yes, it is common today to refer to a church building as a "church," but we know that the Bible has something different in mind when speaking of the church. The church is also much more than a gathering of Christians. To say the church is "the people, not the building" points us in the right direction, but is still dangerously incomplete.

What makes a local church a church? What are the basic and essential elements that must be in place for a true and healthy church to exist and fulfill the mission given to it by Jesus (see Matt. 28:18–20)? Do three Christians gathered for prayer make up a church? What if they all sing hymns and one of them preaches a sermon? Is it then a church? If they take up an offering and give themselves a name, are they then a church? Perhaps if they file as a 501(c)(3) nonprofit organization they are finally a church. In truth, a local church is much more than even all this.

When the Protestant Reformers found themselves at odds with the Roman Catholic Church—the only church they had ever known—and were excommunicated for their understanding of the gospel, they were forced to seek a scriptural definition and function of the local church. Furthermore, was such a church something they could start?

The Reformers concluded from Scripture that a true church exists where the Word of God is rightly preached and the ordinances rightly administered. These two marks are integral to what it means to be the church, to be sure. But they do not stand alone; they are organically connected to other critical components. To preach and administer the ordinances rightly requires biblical leadership and the proper exercise of church discipline. And it is only through all this that the mission of the church is accomplished.

What the church *is* determines what the church *does*. Unless we grasp what and how God has designed His church to be and function, we are likely to find ourselves moving further and further away from what we should be and what we are called to do.

Scripture uses the term *church* in two distinct ways: of the church universal and the local church.

The church universal is made up of all believers in all areas in all ages. It is sometimes referred to by theologians as the "invisible church" because it is not located in or confined to one city or building. In that sense, the whole cannot be seen visibly.

The 1689 Baptist Confession of Faith teaches this well:

> The catholic or universal church, which (with respect to the internal work of the Spirit and truth of grace) may be called invisible, consists of the whole number of the elect, that have been, are, or shall be gathered into one, under Christ, the head thereof; and is the spouse, the body, the fulness of him that fills all in all.[1]

This invisible church is the body of Christ, who is its Head, ultimate authority, and Savior (Col. 1:18). But when the Bible speaks of the church, it does not speak primarily of it as a universal entity, though it is that indeed. Most often, Scripture focuses on the local church.

The word *church* comes from the Greek word *ekklesia*, which means "assembly." That term can be used to describe any kind of assembly, but when applied to the New Testament church it denotes something unique.

The local church is an assembly of believers in Jesus, united together by a common confession, in one localized body, ruled by Scripture, and working to-gether for the mission given to them by their Lord.

Many New Testament letters were written to specific local churches, addressing issues relevant to them as they followed Christ (1 Cor. 4:14; 2 Cor. 9:1; Jude 3). These churches regularly gathered together for the preaching of the Word, prayer, administration of the ordinances, and the singing of psalms, hymns, and spiritual songs (see 1 Cor. 11:20; Acts 2:42; Col. 3:16). And their unity was expressed in a common confession.

The confession of every local church is simple: Jesus Christ is Lord (Rom. 10:9; Phil. 2:11; 1 John 4:1–3). Beyond that, recited and written confessions have been used by churches throughout history. Paul seems to be handing on a known confession to the church in Corinth when he wrote,

> For I delivered to you as of first importance what I also received: that Christ died for our sins in accordance with the Scriptures, that he was buried, that he was raised on the third day in accordance with the Scriptures, and that he appeared to Cephas, then to the twelve.
>
> (1 COR. 15:3–5)

Throughout church history, Presbyterians, Congregationalists, Lutherans, Baptists, and many others have made use of confessions of faith that summarize the doctrines that unite them together as individual churches and as cooperating churches.

All this serves the mission of the church, to which Jesus has commissioned us.

If a local church is an assembly of united believers on mission, what are the essential components of a church that keep its light shining brightly? What makes for a true and healthy church can be boiled down to five essentials: (1) the right preaching of Scripture, (2) the proper administration of the ordinances, (3) the development of biblical leadership, (4) the gracious implementation of church discipline, and (5) a clear focus on the mission that Jesus gave the church.

PART 1

the WORD RIGHTLY PREACHED

The Word of God gives life to the church of God (Eph. 2:18–20). A church can exist and thrive spiritually only where the Scripture is rightly preached. Organization, programs, and ministers do not make a church. There must be preaching.

Unfortunately, preaching is misunderstood by many churches today. Inspiring messages, practical and down-to-earth "talks," and motivational speeches do not qualify as preaching. Good preaching will always be practical, in the sense that sermons make the connection between the truth of Scripture and the real-life experience of the believer. Preaching that is strong indeed motivates and inspires, but not by virtue of eloquence or emotive stories. Something deep happens when the Word is rightly preached.

To rightly preach the Word is to make known the truth of God from Scripture by exposing men, women, and children to the curse of sin and the hope of the gospel. Scripture is not rightly preached unless the law of God exposes our corruption and condemnation, the grace of God shows us the offer of forgiveness and eternal life, and the ways of God are encouraged in faith and repentance.

There are different ways in which the Word can be rightly preached, but it should always be expository— meaning that the truths contained in a particular passage are communicated by the preacher, emphasizing relevant implications and applications, while ultimately drawing the congregation to see the gospel of Jesus Christ more clearly. Some expositors focus on preaching though entire books of the Bible, verse by verse. This method is beneficial as it helps the church learn how to properly interpret the Bible, while leading them through a variety of theological and practical subjects determined by the Scripture itself. It also forces the church to deal with issues we might otherwise avoid. For example, one cannot preach through Romans without having to wrestle with the complete spiritual depravity of every human being, the exclusivity of salvation in Christ alone, the absolute sovereignty of God in salvation, as well as the nature and necessity of godliness. And one cannot rightly preach the book of Daniel without acknowledging God's rule over all kings and kingdoms of the world, and the life of faith lived in a pagan world.

Yet there is also great value in thematic preaching, in which various passages—often not connected by immediate context—are preached through in an organized series to help us understand broad or complicated truths in the Bible. Thematic series are helpful for unpacking doctrines such as the Trinity, issues like spiritual warfare, or the mission of the church. Thematic preaching also allows pastors to address important issues that the church needs to hear in a direct and concentrated manner.

To preach the Word rightly requires pastors to preach the Scripture alone (*sola Scriptura*), not their own ideas and agendas, and to present the gospel for all to believe. True preaching is not mere commentary on passages of Scripture, but a warning of judgment and a heralding of good news. It convicts and encourages. It not only informs, but also transforms.

Implicit in preaching the Word rightly is the task of

understanding and presenting sound doctrine. We cannot preach the Word rightly unless we understand it rightly. And good theology helps us to understand God as He has revealed Himself in Scripture.

Theology consists of particular truths known as "doctrines." At the heart of a church, and of Christian theology, is the gospel of Jesus Christ—the good news that the Son of God fulfilled all righteousness, died for sinners, and rose from the dead, bringing salvation to all who believe in Him. Such truths are essential not only to know the Lord, but to know ourselves—a double knowledge that makes for healthy Christians and vibrant churches. A church is not a church if it does not confess "the faith that was once for all delivered to the saints" (Jude 3).

A healthy local church is built upon and governed by Scripture. This means we must embrace the Bible's authority, sufficiency, and usefulness.

Chapter 1

THE BIBLE'S AUTHORITY

The Bible is unlike any other book. There are thousands of sacred texts used by various religious groups searching for wisdom and life. But the Bible stands out from the rest, not only in terms of the number of ancient copies that have survived throughout history and its popularity around the world, but also in terms of what it is. The Bible is not merely the words of spiritual leaders or a book of instruction. It is the very Word of God.

THE BIBLE'S DIVINE ORIGIN

When the apostle Paul explains that "all Scripture is breathed out by God" (2 Tim. 3:16), he is telling us that what the church recognized to be and received as Holy Scripture, though penned by men, was in fact

God's Word to us. Further, the apostle Peter explains that Scripture is not the invention of man, but that "men spoke from God as they were carried along by the Holy Spirit" (2 Peter 1:20).

Because the Bible has a divine origin, it has divine authority. Psalm 19 unpacks the nature of Scripture and what it accomplishes in the believer:

> The law of the LORD is perfect,
>   reviving the soul;
> the testimony of the LORD is sure,
>   making wise the simple;
> the precepts of the LORD are right,
>   rejoicing the heart;
> the commandment of the LORD is pure,
>   enlightening the eyes;
> the fear of the LORD is clean,
>   enduring forever;
> the rules of the LORD are true,
>   and righteous altogether.
> More to be desired are they than gold,
>   even much fine gold;
> sweeter also than honey
>   and drippings of the honeycomb.
> Moreover, by them is your servant warned;
>   in keeping them there is great reward.
>
> (PS. 19:7–11)

Scripture is "perfect," meaning that it is complete and lacking in nothing regarding its teaching on Christian faith and practice. While we profit from the preaching and writing of Christian leaders, only when they rightly understand and apply Scripture do we benefit spiritually. The Bible is perfect.

Scripture is "sure," meaning that it is trustworthy. Theologians often talk about "the trustworthiness of Scripture," meaning that the Bible is reliable in all that it teaches. When people bet on horses—I am not advocating gambling—a "sure thing" is a horse that is guaranteed to win. Your bet is safe. There will be a return on your investment. Of course, there is no such thing as a "sure thing" in the matters of the world. But when it comes to the Bible, we have the divine promise that it is sure. And all of its promises are reliable. We cannot lose by believing what it teaches.

Scripture is "right," meaning that it communicates the person, work, and will of God. It is in full accord with who God is and what He wants from us and for us. While God is unknowable in any complete way since He is infinite and eternal, we have the assurance that what the Bible reveals about God is right. It is not spiritual guesswork.

Scripture is "pure" in that it is without corruption in its content and message. We believe that the Word of God is "inerrant," meaning that it contains no errors in whatever it teaches. And beyond that, the Word of God is pure in its morality. Many today believe that the ethics and doctrines communicated in the Bible are not only primitive and antiquated, but also are immoral. How can a God condemning someone to hell be good? How can punishment for sin we inherited be just? How can the Bible teach that true marriage is between one man and one woman, and anything outside of that is sinful? Biblical morality is perceived to be out of step with our culture and "common sense" and thus impure. But the standard of righteousness is not found in the convictions of any one human, nor in the general consensus of any society. The standard of righteousness is found only in the God who created all things. He alone is pure, and His word is pure (1 John 1:5).

Scripture is "clean," meaning that it is not only pure in itself, but also that it purifies all who receive it by faith. Scripture is the instrument by which God cleanses a soul and sanctifies a spirit (Eph. 5:26). It keeps us from sin, calls us to Christ, is the means by which we are born again (1 Peter 1:23), and is what God uses to transform us from the inside out (Rom. 12:2).

Scripture is "true," just as God is true and Jesus is "the truth" (John 14:6). Despite what the world tells us today, truth exists and can be known. We can discover much of it, but the most important truth is that which we cannot unearth on our own. It has been revealed by

God Himself. He has opened the deepest mysteries of life and death, God and humanity, eternity and salvation, in the pages of Holy Scripture. So when we open the Book, we open something given to us by God that is complete, trustworthy, comprehensive, life-changing, and true. All of this means that it brings with it authority which we all must recognize.

THE BIBLE'S CLAIM

Today in our Western individualistic culture, we tend to bristle at the idea of authority, unless it is our own. Most of us say we like freedom, but what we really want is radical autonomy—a life lived independently from the authority of another. We want to live life our way and for our own purposes. And when it comes to spirituality, most prefer anarchy to order and creativity to confession. But the Bible, as the Word of God, rightly claims a position of authority in the life of the church.

As Christians, we may be quick to say that God is our authority, but we must say more than that. If we say that the Lord is our God, then we must also say that His Word is authoritative in the church and in our own lives. This second confession is more difficult to make, for it means that there is a clearly articulated authority that directly applies to our thoughts, decisions, and actions, and to which we are held accountable.

The authority of Scripture implies that we should hear and accept God's Word as indeed divine when it is read and preached. Not only that, we should heed it as His very message to us. Every time we open Scripture to read it, we must recognize that God has spoken, and that He is speaking today—to us. It is all too easy to treat the Bible as a text to study and know, only to forget that it has been given to us so that we may be confronted by the God who wrote it, convicted of the sin it condemns, and rescued by the grace it offers to all. The authoritative Word of God, the Bible, is God's Word to us, and we must receive it as such.

Many people want a special word from the Lord, to have one of those miraculous moments when His voice breaks through the clouds and echoes overhead in booming authority. But we have something better: the voice of God recorded perfectly on pages that, when read, echoes in our hearts with thundering certainty. The miracle stays with us, and its authority is a gift and a safeguard. The old Baptist confession gives us a beautiful summary of this truth:

> The Holy Scripture is the only sufficient, certain, and infallible rule of all saving knowledge, faith, and obedience, although the light of nature, and the works of creation and providence do so far manifest the goodness, wisdom, and power of God, as to leave men

inexcusable; yet they are not sufficient to give that knowledge of God and His will which is necessary unto salvation. Therefore it pleased the Lord at sundry times and in diversified manners to reveal Himself, and to declare (that) His will unto His church; and afterward for the better preserving and propagating of the truth, and for the more sure establishment and comfort of the church against the corruption of the flesh, and the malice of Satan, and of the world, to commit the same wholly unto writing; which makes the Holy Scriptures to be most necessary, those former ways of God's revealing His will unto His people being now completed.[2]

No doubt, a local church should be governed by elders working with the congregation. But the final evaluation of all that is done in and through the church is the Scripture itself.

Chapter 2

THE BIBLE'S SUFFICIENCY

When we say that the Bible is authoritative, we mean that it is the ultimate word in all faith and practice. Not only do we take it seriously; it takes us by the hand and leads us in all areas of life. We submit to it, rejoice in it, and shape our lives according to it. While many churches today embrace the authority of God's Word, they are tempted to keep their distance from its sufficiency.

SCRIPTURE IS ENOUGH

When we say that Scripture is sufficient, we mean that it is enough. It is all we need to know God and to maintain a vital relationship with Him by faith. We need nothing more than Holy Scripture to organize our churches and to order our lives. This does not mean that if a specific way of making disciples is not found with a chapter and verse it is out of place in the church. Local churches are tasked with making disciples through the preaching and teaching of the Word. Outside of corporate worship, we may choose to gather for Bible study or to develop Sunday school classes as other means of carrying on the mission. All we need to make disciples is found in Scripture, though we may use practical wisdom in applying the best methods for carrying out what Scripture commands.

During the Reformation, men like Martin Luther objected to the Roman Catholic Church's stance on matters of authority in the church. For Catholics, Scripture was but one authority. Equal to it were both church traditions and the pope's teachings. The Reformers objected, arguing that contradictions and errors, which could not be inspired by God, could be found in these authorities. Instead, they taught "Scripture alone" (*sola Scriptura* in Latin), meaning that Scripture is the final authority by which all other teachings must be judged.

This does not mean, however, that we cannot benefit from the writings of Christian men and women through the ages. We should indeed seek out such individuals who help us to better grasp the meaning and significance of Scripture. But Scripture must be considered the final arbiter of truth and the standard by which we evaluate all teachings, sermons, and books. Most importantly, it means that only Scripture has the power to change the heart and transform the soul. The further we move away from the authority and sufficiency of Scripture, the weaker our churches become—not only in focus, but also in fruitfulness. The Bible is sufficient in that it teaches us all we need to know about God, His precepts, and His promises. It alone instructs us in the way we are to live as God's people.

KNOWING GOD

God cannot be known in His entirety by finite and fallen humanity. He is too big, and we are too small, for us to fully comprehend all that He is. But what can be known of God is revealed in the Bible. So that is where we look to understand Him and His ways. No one can develop an accurate picture of who God is through mere reason or imagination. Such things, apart from the Bible, leave us with a god of our own making. But as we read through the pages of Scripture, we can begin to see some of our Maker. The Bible tells us that God is a spirit who is infinite, eternal, and unchangeable in His being wisdom, power, holiness, justice, goodness, and truth.[1]

When God speaks of Himself to Moses in the book of Exodus, He describes Himself as

*merciful and gracious, slow to anger, and abound-
ing in steadfast love and faithfulness, keeping
steadfast love for thousands, forgiving iniquity and
transgression and sin, but who will by no means
clear the guilty, visiting the iniquity of the fathers on
the children and the children's children, to the third
and the fourth generation.*

(EX. 34:6–7)

God is both just and merciful. He must punish sin, but He also forgives. Many people tend to think of God as one or the other, but He is eternally and perfectly both, and only Scripture helps us understand that this is true.

God tells us who He is and what He does in His Word. God is holy, all-powerful, all-knowing, and all-present. He is an active God who oversees all the details of our lives. He is eternally triune, existing as Father, Son, and Holy Spirit. We can know these things and more because God, in His kindness, has revealed them to us in His Word.

And God's revelation is not merely a list of propositions. Rather, He used a variety of literary forms to help us understand Him. From poetry to proverbs, from narratives to letters, from parables to prophecy—God has revealed Himself to us in ways that we can understand.

Those who want to know who God is and what He is like will find the answer only in the pages of Holy Scripture. The revelation of God in the Bible is not given so that we might simply learn information about Him, but that we would know Him by faith and enter into a right relationship with Him through His Son, Jesus Christ. The Word was given so that we would love God, glorify Him, and enjoy Him in both this life and the one to come.

KNOWING GOD'S PRECEPTS

The Bible reveals who God is and what His will and ways are. And these are revealed in His commands, also called His "law," which should be seen as a gift. In telling us what God requires of us, and in showing us the way we are to live, He has not left us in the dark wondering what is morally right and wrong. We do not have to establish our own code by which to live. Instead, we have a divine directive that shows us the right way.

In Scripture, the term *law* can refer to the first five books of the Old Testament, the whole Old Testament itself, the commands given to Israel in the Old Covenant, just the Ten Commandments, or the binding commands of God relevant at any given time. What we are considering at the present are the commands of God relevant to us as God's people.

The law, or God's precepts, are given to us for practical, not theoretical, purposes. One purpose is to show us the way of righteousness. His law is a godly rule for all of life and should be obeyed by all people. In this sense, the law is always holy, just, and good (Rom. 7:12).

But there is another, primary, purpose of the law: to expose our sinfulness and show us our need for a Savior. While the law is good, we are not. We have not kept God's commands. Instead, we have both carelessly wandered away from His ways and outright rejected them whenever they have not suited our interests. The law of God shows us that all have sinned and fallen short of God's glory (Rom 3:23; 7:7–11). The law not only instructs, but also reveals and condemns our disobedience. The law shows us what is right, what is wrong, and what is needed.[2] God's law prepares us to receive the good news of the gospel.

KNOWING GOD'S PROMISES

If the precepts of God—His law—show us the way of righteousness and reveal our unrighteousness and deserved condemnation, then the promises of God show us that there is mercy to be received. God in His kindness offers to sinners grace by which we can be forgiven and reconciled to Him.

From Genesis to Revelation, the promises of God center on the person and work of Jesus Christ. He is the one who would fulfill all righteousness, conquer our enemies, and rescue us from death. And this gift of salvation and deliverance, which is offered to all, is received by faith alone. For Abraham and Peter, for you and me, God's promises are free for the taking.

Consider the promises of God: a Conqueror will come to crush the devil (Gen. 3:15), a King will come to reign over us all in peace and righteousness (2 Sam. 7:12–13), and a Savior will come to take away all our sin and guilt (Isa. 53). He promises to forget our sins (Isa. 43:25), give us new hearts, and cause us to walk in His ways (Ezek. 36: 25–27). He promises to be with us, to reside within us (John 14:15–17), and never to forsake us (Heb. 13:5). Apart from the promises of God, the precepts of God plague us. For only by grace can we begin to live according to God's ways. But with the promises of God, the precepts protect and purify us.

The Bible is both authoritative and sufficient. A true church believes and rests upon the Scripture alone, and by the Scripture our lives and our churches are established.

Chapter 3

THE BIBLE'S
USEFULNESS

The Bible is not a book of arcane philosophies or moral tales, but a truly spiritual book, *the* Book, that is living, active, and powerful (Heb. 4:12). It is both transformative and useful in the life of every believer. The apostle Paul gives us four uses that result in spiritual maturity and readiness for the work God has called us to:

> *All Scripture is breathed out by God and profitable for* teaching, *for* reproof, *for* correction, *and for* training *in righteousness, that the man of God may be complete, equipped for every good work.*
>
> (2 TIM. 3:16–17; *emphasis added*)

Apart from the Bible, maturity and readiness will remain something in the distance that we long for but never experience.

TEACHING

The Bible is useful for teaching. Paul uses this term frequently in his pastoral epistles to urge ministers in the use of the Scripture for its divinely given purpose. Scripture was not given only to be read, but also to be explained, applied, and received by faith. God has given us His Word so that by it we might be instructed in the knowledge of God and in the Christian life. All Scripture is inspired by God, and part of its usefulness is in teaching us what we are to believe and how we are to live.

The doctrines of creation, sin, salvation, and the future are not incidental concepts that we should treat lightly. Rather, our thinking of these topics should be formed, and constantly reformed, by the Word of God. Who God is and what He has done, is doing, and will do must all be determined by Scripture alone. Who we are and what we are made to become are truths so deep and important that we cannot allow our imagination to lead us. Scripture was given to instruct us in all of this and more. This means that our posture toward the Word must be that of a learner. We come to it seeking knowledge and wisdom that can be found only in the pages of Holy Scripture.

The church is tasked with the sacred privilege of instruction, which means that a church is appointed by God to teach doctrine and devotion. Unfortunately, many churches tend to lean toward one or the other, focusing on either theology or Christian living. It is common to find some churches that are deeply invested in doctrine yet remain weak in promoting Christian piety. Other churches emphasize the experiential aspect of our faith without digging into the theology that is necessary for true, grounded experience.

Theology and experience cannot be separated. Each is incomplete without the other. Doctrine without devotion is empty knowledge, and devotion without doctrine is superficial emotion. The local church cannot fulfill the Great Commission apart from teaching, for this is the primary means by which disciples are made.

Implicit in Paul's call to teach, and stated explicitly elsewhere in Scripture, is the responsibility of the church to guard against false doctrine and heresy. Faulty theology and damnable doctrine have been working their way into the midst of God's people since the garden of Eden. If the local church is not a teaching church, then the people of God are left unprepared for their mission and the challenges of life, and exposed to dangers that can shipwreck one's faith.

REPROOF

The Bible tells us not only what is true, but also what is wrong. In doing so, it convicts us of sin. Scripture is able to accomplish far more than the persuasive words of any man or woman. It has the ability to uncover our doubt, jealousy, hatred, lust, and pride. God's Word is sharper than any two-edged sword and can penetrate deep into the soul to reveal what is in the heart (Heb. 4:12). Such reproof is necessary to every Christian's life, since we are called to daily repent of our sins and trust in Jesus Christ. Apart from the ministry of the Word, our sins are underexposed, leaving our lives underdeveloped.

Reproof, though, is not just the result of our reading Scripture or hearing it taught; it is also the responsibility of brothers and sisters in Christ when sin has gotten the better of us. Proverbs 19:25 tells us to "reprove a man of understanding, and he will gain knowledge."

Churches sometimes mistake the call to reprove with the worldly tactic of shaming. Reproof is not putting the moral screws to another until they admit they are wrong and sorry. The church's aim is not to shame an individual, but to steer them clear of danger so that they may flourish in faith. Reproof requires that we point to both the danger of sin and the deliverance we have in Jesus. It is incomplete if we do not take people by the hand and lead them back to Christ. James tells us, "Whoever brings back a sinner from his wandering will save his soul from death and will cover a multitude of sins" (James 5:20).

While reproof is seldom fruitful apart from having an established relationship with someone, it is never fruitful apart from the use of Scripture. Those who walk in the light while fleeing the darkness of sin will embrace reproof as a means of spiritual growth.

CORRECTION

While reproof points out sin and calls for repentance, correction reorients a person to the way he or she ought to think and live. Correction is necessary for everyone because each of us sins in our daily living and err in our understanding of God. What else can direct our minds, hearts, and hands successfully but the perfect Word of God? When we have a small view of God, believing that He can do nothing for us in the midst our trouble, Scripture challenges and changes us. When we seek satisfaction in ourselves and in sin rather than in Christ and godliness, we will only be convicted and corrected by the voice of God speaking directly to us in His Word.

Correction, like reproof, does not happen simply when one reads the Bible. It often comes through the love and ministry of others who speak the Word to us and show us a better way. Sometimes by example and often by words given at the right time, we are reoriented to the truth and made right in our thinking. Those who desire to have both good theology and a growing faith will be open to the correction that comes from the Scripture by means of the people God has put in our lives.

And this requires much of us. Cain was wrong when he presumed he was not his brother's keeper (Gen. 4:9). We are indeed our brother's and sister's keeper. This aspect of Scripture's usefulness is true for all believers, not just pastors. All of us are called to "encourage one another" in the church (1 Thess. 5:11).

TRAINING IN RIGHTEOUSNESS

The Bible instructs us, rebukes us, corrects us, and trains us in godly living. God wants not just right thinking of us, but also right living. He is glorified in us when we know Him (theology) and live for Him (godliness).

Just as an athlete is trained to run, swim, jump, hit, or throw by means of trainers, equipment, and discipline, so the church is trained in righteousness by means of Scripture. Training in righteousness is not external conformity to religious practices, but the progressive work of killing sin and obeying the Lord.

A popular notion today suggests that our growth in the grace of godliness is more about "letting go and letting God" than that of "working out" our salvation (Phil. 2:12) by the obedience of faith. Some have wrongly concluded that trying to be godly will cause us to focus on godliness over God, that if we put effort in our own sanctification we are taking our eyes off the Savior. This is not only a false dichotomy; it is unbiblical.

While we have no inherent power to make ourselves godly, we are called to "train" ourselves for godliness, knowing that such activity holds promise for the present life and for the life to come (1 Tim. 4:7). God not only commands us to work, strive, and obey, but also supplies the power necessary to do these—and well. Paul teaches,

> *Therefore, my beloved, as you have always obeyed,*
> *so now, not only as in my presence but much more*
> *in my absence, work out your own salvation with*
> *fear and trembling, for it is God who works in you,*
> *both to will and to work for his good pleasure.*
>
> (PHIL. 2:12–13)

God is at work in His people to become what He created us to be. He is the one conforming us to the image of His Son. But we are participants with Him in that work, as we are "doers of the word" (James 1:23–25), "work heartily" (Col. 3:23–24), and supplement our faith with virtue (2 Peter 1:5).

Our training is in accordance with the Word, in response to the Word, and in the power of the Word. And it is in the context of the church that we would be trained in righteousness.

All of this is demonstrates that the Bible is useful, and

therefore eminently relevant, to the church and life of faith today. It is common today to see churches attempt to make the Bible "relevant." From bad reimaginings of Scripture that are not actual translations to the mishandling of the Word by turning it into a how-to book of improved living, the church obscures the actual relevance of Scripture. The Bible cannot be made relevant, for it is already relevant to every man, woman, and child alive. In fact, the Bible reveals that apart from the truth contained in it, there is no relevance to be found in this life. It is all vanity and a chasing after the wind (see Eccl. 1–2).

A true church is not only Bible-believing, but also Bible-dependent and Bible-governed. It rightly preaches the Word because only the Word of God has the authority and power needed to give life and growth to God's people.

PART 2

the
ORDINANCES
RIGHTLY
ADMINISTERED

Jesus gave the church two ordinances, or sacraments, to be administered to the body as a symbolic preaching of the gospel for the nurturing of our faith and as a means of maintaining communion with Him. Baptism and the Lord's Supper are sacred traditions given to us by Jesus Himself and by which we draw near to Him in faith.

To rightly administer the ordinances of baptism and the Lord's Supper means that we offer them to the church as a sign and symbol of the gospel. They do not save; nor are the elements—water, bread, and wine—magical. Yet something spiritual and mysterious occurs when we are baptized and receive the Lord's Supper. For the word *sacrament*—from the Latin *sacramentum,* derived from the Greek term *mysterion*—means "mystery."

Both terms, *sacraments* and *ordinances,* are acceptable, though my tradition—Baptist—prefers to use *ordinance.* The words are generally interchangeable, though they have different emphases. To call the Lord's Supper an "ordinance," for instance, emphasizes its formal place and significance in the life of a church. To call it a "sacrament" emphasizes its divine and sacred origin, and the mysterious aspect of Christ's presence with His people when they gather around the Word and sacrament.

—

Chapter 4

BAPTIZED IN THE NAME OF THE FATHER, SON, AND HOLY SPIRIT

Just before Jesus ascended into heaven, He told His apostles,

> *Go therefore and make disciples of all nations, baptizing them in the name of the Father and of the Son and of the Holy Spirit, teaching them to observe all that I have commanded you. And behold, I am with you always, to the end of the age.*

(MATT. 28:19–20)

Jesus calls the church to baptize those who are disciples. One of the two ordinances that Jesus gave the church as symbols of the gospel, baptism is a means of confessing Christ and a means of grace. Baptism is the immersion of a believer in water, in the name of the Father, Son, and Holy Spirit. It marks a person as belonging to Christ.

To properly understand baptism, we need to see it as a symbol and as a testimony.

A SYMBOL

Baptism is a picture of the salvation found in Jesus Christ, a symbol of the redemption accomplished through His death and resurrection. One picture it sets forth is that of washing, or cleansing from sin. Just as water cleanses the body, so Christ cleanses His people.

Baptism is also a picture of the believer's union with Christ and our spiritual death and resurrection:

> *Do you not know that all of us who have been baptized into Christ Jesus were baptized into his death? We were buried therefore with him by baptism into death, in order that, just as Christ was raised from the dead by the glory of the Father, we too might walk in newness of life.*
>
> (ROM. 6:3–4)

The believer is inseparably united to Jesus and now finds her identity in the Savior. Baptism attests to this reality. Just as Jesus was buried and raised from death, so we have been dead and made alive in Him. Our baptism depicts this in dramatic fashion as we are submerged in water and brought up from its depths (Gal. 3:27; Col. 2:12–13).

The mode of baptism is important because, as an aspect of obedience and worship, we seek to follow the instructions and pattern given to us in the Scripture. And what we find in Scripture, demonstrated by the early church, is immersion (Mark 1:5; John 3:23; Acts 8:36–38).

A TESTIMONY

Baptism is not a picture of a potential salvation, but of salvation received. It is a testimony, not of one's future faith, but of Christ's accomplished redemption and an individual's union with Him. Baptism is for those the Lord has called to Himself and who have received the Word (Acts 2:38–41).

Many Bible-believing and theologically rich churches practice infant baptism: the children of believing parents are sprinkled with water as a sign of the salvation promised to them and of their membership in the covenant community. These brothers and sisters do not believe that baptism saves, but that it is a sign of salvation and that it points toward the future faith of children yet to be converted. They also see a close connection between the old covenant sign of circumcision and the new covenant sign of baptism. We, however, are not persuaded by this perspective, as the recipients of baptism in Scripture are those who call on the name of the Lord. The new covenant, different from the old covenant, is made up exclusively of believers (see Heb. 8). Baptism testifies that one has believed in Christ and is now—by faith, and not by baptism—a member of the new covenant. As Paul explains,

> In him also you were circumcised with a circumcision made without hands, by putting off the body of the flesh, by the circumcision of Christ, having been buried with him in baptism, in which you were also raised with him through faith in the powerful working of God, who raised him from the dead.
>
> (COL. 2:11–12)

Baptism is also a testimony of our partnership in the church. Generally, baptism is connected to a local congregation and membership in that church. We all share in one baptism and are a part of one body:

> There is one body and one Spirit—just as you were called to the one hope that belongs to your call—one Lord, one faith, one baptism, one God and Father of all, who is over all and through all and in all.
>
> (EPH. 4:4–6)

Baptism tells a story of Christ's work and our conversion. Baptism properly administered is the immersion of a believer in water, in the name of the Father, Son, and Holy Spirit. As a kind of preaching of the gospel and confession of Jesus Christ, baptism is a public ordinance performed by the church before witnesses. Location and timing is less important than who is baptized and how. But this is not a private ceremony. This is a church ordinance, and is therefore intended to bless the entire congregation. In it, the gospel is preached to all present, and the work of God in an individual's life is celebrated by all.

A MEANS OF GRACE

Although baptism does not save, it preaches the gospel, announces the truth of Jesus Christ, and as such is a means of grace when received by faith. The water does not cleanse or sanctify; only Christ does that. But as we rest upon the truth proclaimed in baptism, we draw near to God, and He draws near to us. In this ordinance, we encounter God's grace and are truly sanctified.

Baptism is not merely a religious rite with rich symbolism. It is one of the means that God uses to work in us and make us who we are in Christ.

Chapter 5

—

CHRIST'S BODY BROKEN AND BLOOD SPILLED

The night before Jesus was betrayed by Judas, He celebrated the Passover with His disciples. After the meal had concluded, Jesus took bread, broke it, and told the disciples, "This is my body, which is given for you. Do this in remembrance of me" (Luke 22:19). He then took wine, distributed it among the disciples, and said, "This cup that is poured out for you is the new covenant in my blood" (Luke 22:20). In that moment, Jesus gave the church a sacred tradition that is to be observed until He returns (1 Cor. 11:26).

Jesus gave us this ordinance in order to remember Him and His work, and in doing so to draw near to Him by faith. This is no empty ritual or mere formality. It is a spiritual means by which we are sanctified and Christ draws near to us.

The bread and the wine themselves are not the means of grace. Simply drinking the cup and eating the bread brings God's blessing to no one. Rather, grace is conveyed through the gospel message presented by and with the elements when received by faith. As the 1689 Second London Confession of Faith puts it,

> Worthy receivers, outwardly partaking of the visible elements in this ordinance, do then also inwardly by faith, really and indeed, yet not carnally and corporally, but spiritually receive, and feed upon Christ crucified, and all the benefits of his death; the body and blood of Christ being then not corporally or carnally, but spiritually present to the faith of believers in that ordinance, as the elements themselves are to their outward senses.[1]

Receiving the Lord's Supper in a proper manner means trusting in the promises given to us in Jesus and drawing near to Him by faith. As a result, we are blessed and enter into a special fellowship with Him.

In 1 Corinthians, the apostle Paul says, "The cup of blessing that we bless, is it not a participation in the blood of Christ? The bread that we break, is it not a participation in the body of Christ?" (10:16) Commenting on this text, pastor and writer Richard Barcellos argues, "The point being made from this text is that bread and wine are signs which signify present participation or present communion in the present benefits procured by Christ's body and blood."[2] Further, James P. Boyce, founder of the Southern Baptist Theological Seminary in Louisville, Kentucky, explained that the Lord's Supper conveys grace as it communicates the truth of the gospel and is received by faith.[3] The grace we receive is experienced through our vital and immediate fellowship with the Lord.

The blessings made available in the Supper are not stored up for us in heaven for the future. They are not blessings to be enjoyed once we get to where Christ is. Instead, it is as if heaven has been and is being brought to our souls by the Holy Spirit due to the work of Christ in accordance with the Father's electing and predestinating purpose.[4] As we participate in Christ through this ordinance, we are truly sanctified and made more alive in Him.

While the Lord's Supper is indeed a memorial, it is also a spiritual participation, or fellowship, with Jesus. God is at work in the ordinance. He brings blessing to those who take it in faith and discipline or judgment upon those who take it unworthily (we will discuss this more in the next chapter).

When we come to the Lord's Table, we are to come humble and happy, for there we know that God waits to bless us as we commune with His Son.

PLACE AND FREQUENCY

The frequency with which we take the Lord's Supper is one to soberly consider, especially in light of our tendency to do what we have always done. Many churches share in the Lord's Supper infrequently because Scripture does not explicitly prescribe the frequency with which we are to take it. But there are good reasons to include the Lord's Supper in every weekly gathering of corporate worship: the example of the New Testament church, the importance of all the essential elements of biblical worship, and the spiritual benefit it affords all who partake in it.

While Jesus commanded that we simply observe communion "often," the church in the book of Acts seemed to share in it on every Lord's Day: "And they devoted themselves to the apostles' teaching and the fellowship, to the breaking of bread and the prayers" (Acts 2:42).

In Acts 2, the early church devoted themselves to Scripture, prayer, the communion of the saints, and the Lord's Supper (breaking of bread). These were regular practices of the early church, and the church was known to gather most frequently on "the Lord's Day." And Acts 20:7 tells us that breaking bread normally occurred on the first day of the every week: "On the first day of the week, when we were gathered together to break bread, Paul talked with them, intending to depart on the next day, and he prolonged his speech until midnight."

The example of the early church can help inform our practices in the twenty-first century. Yet some question: "Won't taking the Lord's Supper every week rob us of its significance? Isn't there a risk of it becoming a superficial ritual?"

These are good questions. That we all value the Lord's Supper as something special, sacred really, warrants caution in making any changes. However, when we consider all the essential and biblical components of worship, the Lord's Supper stands out as the only one that churches do not do weekly. The reading and preaching of the Word, prayers, spiritual songs and hymns, the offering, and so on are all included in a church's liturgy every week, yet they do not lose their significance. The question ought to be, "Why *don't* we take the Lord's Supper weekly?" It is commanded to be observed frequently by God's people. It naturally belongs in the regular corporate worship of the church on the Lord's Day.

Additionally, if church members are out of town or sick on the Sunday of a church's monthly observance of the Lord's Supper, it could be a long time before they can join the fellowship at the table. Observing the Lord's Supper weekly ensures that all the people are frequently joined together for this sacred tradition. Charles Spurgeon testifies,

I think I speak the mind of many of God's people now present, that coming as some of us do, weekly, to the Lord's table, we do not find the breaking of bread to have lost its significance—it is always fresh to us. . . . They who once know the sweetness of each Lord's-day celebrating his Supper, will not be content, I am sure, to put it off to less frequent seasons. Beloved, when the Holy Ghost is with us, ordinances are wells to the Christian, wells of rich comfort and of near communion.[5]

Chapter 6

—

FENCING THE TABLE

The Lord's Supper is a spiritually significant event, and approaching it in the wrong manner can have dire consequences. In the Corinthian church, the ordinance was marked by various sins, and God brought discipline upon some of the people. Paul writes,

> But in the following instructions I do not commend you, because when you come together it is not for the better but for the worse. For, in the first place, when you come together as a church, I hear that there are divisions among you. And I believe it in part, for there must be factions among you in order that those who are genuine among you may be recognized. When you come together, it is not the Lord's supper that you eat. For in eating, each one goes ahead with his own meal. One goes hungry, another gets drunk. What! Do you not have houses to eat and drink in? Or do you despise the church of

> God and humiliate those who have nothing? What
> shall I say to you? Shall I commend you in this? No,
> I will not. . . .
>
> Whoever, therefore, eats the bread or drinks the cup
> of the Lord in an unworthy manner will be guilty
> concerning the body and blood of the Lord. Let
> a person examine himself, then, and so eat of the
> bread and drink of the cup. For anyone who eats
> and drinks without discerning the body eats and
> drinks judgment on himself. That is why many of
> you are weak and ill, and some have died.
>
> (1 COR. 11:17–22, 27–30)

Eating the bread and drinking the cup in an unworthy manner meant doing so thoughtlessly, faithlessly, without genuine love for others, and without repentance. On account of this, the Lord brought sickness and even death upon some of the parties involved. Not only must a believer examine himself and prepare himself for the Lord's Supper, the church must warn and protect the people who are in the gathering so that may be ready to eat, drink, and remember in a worthy manner. This is called "fencing the table."

Fencing the table is protecting people from partaking of the Lord's Supper in an unworthy manner. This includes receiving it as an unbeliever, an unrepentant believer, and a member of the church currently under restrictive church discipline (we will discuss discipline in detail in part 4). First Corinthians tells us that eating in such a manner can lead to severe discipline and even judgment from the Lord.

Fencing the table is done primarily through public exhortation and warning. So, an elder may say something like:

> Brothers and sisters, this table is prepared for you who have been forgiven of your sins through faith in Jesus Christ. Our Lord gave this sacred tradition to us, His church. It is a gift to sinners who are also believers. You should not think that you can come forward only if you are perfect. Jesus alone is perfect, and He is your perfection. You are invited to come broken, but hopeful, believing and repenting.
>
> If you are not a Christian, you should not receive the bread and the cup. This meal is only for those who have received Jesus by faith. We encourage you to use this time to consider the offer of forgiveness and eternal life that Jesus holds out to all who are willing to receive Him. Place your hope in Him. You might not come forward for communion today, but you can come to Jesus today and find eternal life, which is what all of this is about.

A church does not need to have bouncers near the table, ready to toss out those who should not partake. The warning is typically enough. If the elders believe that someone has taken the Lord's Supper in an unworthy manner, they should follow up with the individual afterward to gain better insight to what was happening so they may know how to best shepherd them. If someone currently under restrictive church discipline came forward, then one of the elders should walk up beside them and ask them to step aside to talk through the issue and their heart. To some, this may seem overbearing, but such action is done in love and with the well-being of the person in mind.

WHO CAN PARTAKE?

Are the only prerequisites for receiving the Lord's Supper faith and repentance, or is there more? In Baptist circles, three views vie for who can receive the Supper: closed, close, and open communion. These positions do not address the spiritual readiness of individuals, but rather focus on the stewardship of church authority and fencing the table.

Closed Communion

This practice admits only members of that particular local church to the Lord's Supper. Thus, visitors from other churches cannot partake. These churches fence the table by limiting the meal to those they know, covenant with, and who are accountable to the leadership.

Close Communion

Only believers who have been baptized by immersion are admitted to the Supper. This means those Christians who have been baptized as infants, or as a believer by some practice other than immersion—that is, pouring or sprinkling—are not admitted to the table. These churches believe that baptism must precede taking communion, and that baptism necessarily means immersion of those confessing Jesus personally. Therefore, those who have not been properly baptized are not ready for the second ordinance.

Open Communion

All who have trusted in Jesus Christ are admitted to the table. Differences in views on the mode of baptism, therefore, does not restrict them from receiving the meal. All who know the Lord and are "visible saints" are welcome to participate in communion. In his classic *Differences in Water Baptism, No Bar to Communion*, John Bunyan explains, "The church of Christ hath not warrant to keep out of their communion the Christian that is discovered to be a visible saint by the word, the Christian that walketh according to his light with God."[1]

Bunyan argued that in spite of our differences in secondary issues, our unity as Christians compels us to unite in the preaching and receiving of the Word of

God—verbally and sacramentally. If it is true that "there is one body and one Spirit . . . one hope . . . one Lord, one faith, one baptism, one God and Father of all, who is over all and through all and in all" (Eph. 4:4–6), then how can we forbid brothers and sisters with whom we share all of this from partaking of the Lord's Supper?

Healthy, biblical churches may hold to any of these three options, but I am convinced that John Bunyan is correct and that open communion with other believers best reflects what is demonstrated in Scripture.

However the church fences the table—and every church should—they should do so clearly, graciously, and always with the offer for people to believe in Jesus Christ. Only those who are ready to partake by faith are ready for the Lord's Supper.

PARTAKING BY FAITH

The Lord's Supper, or Communion, is a sacred tradition. During the Passover meal with His disciples, Jesus blessed us with an ordinance that, through the elements of bread and wine, the gospel is preached, our faith is encouraged, and the church is united in familial love. The 1689 Confession explains,

> The supper of the Lord Jesus was instituted by him the same night wherein he was betrayed, to be observed

in his churches, unto the end of the world, for the perpetual remembrance, and showing to all the world the sacrifice of himself in his death, confirmation of the faith of believers in all the benefits thereof, their spiritual nourishment, and growth in him, their further engagement in, and to all duties which they owe to him; and to be a bond and pledge of their communion with him, and with each other.[2]

Before we receive this meal, we would be wise to ask ourselves if we are ready. This may seem odd, but preparation and self-examination are important to taking the meal aright (1 Cor. 11:28–31).

When should you not take communion? If you remain unrepentant of sin and are refusing to deny yourself, take up your cross, and follow Jesus, you should remain seated. Taking communion in such a condition is a form of hypocrisy that while hidden, hardens the heart.

Unfortunately, however, many Christians treat the Lord's Supper as an overly introspective and nearly depressing act. Some are encouraged to so focus on their sin that, despite the beautiful gospel proclamation in the Supper, the joy of salvation is nowhere to be found. In fact, some believers will decide not to participate at all because they believe they have messed up too badly. They see the table and hear the invitation, but fear they should not go forward because the past week was filled with sin and unbelief.

But just as Jesus came to call not the righteous but sinners to repentance (Luke 5:32), so He invites us sinners to His table. If you come to the assembly unrepentant and doubting, you have time to repent and commit yourself again to Jesus. We should come to the table believing, confessing our sin, turning from it, and trusting the gospel promises afresh. We come to the table *simul iustus et peccator*—simultaneously justified and a sinner. Knowing and resting in God's sovereign pardon of sinners produces joy and leads to worship.

As you examine yourself and find yourself to be sinful and in need of mercy, know that you have found it in Jesus. Come to the table, humbled by your sin and happy in your Savior. There you will find grace.

PART 3

LEADERSHIP BIBLICALLY FORMED and FUNCTIONING

Leaders in the church today all too often lack transparency and accountability, and are domineering. The church of Jesus Christ does not simply need leaders; she needs good leaders—godly men who shepherd faithfully while denying themselves. The leadership of a church cannot be merely a board of directors who make decisions, but a fellowship of shepherds who care for God's people.

Churches generally do not lack in leadership, but many lack in leadership that is biblically formed and functional. This means that the primary offices within the church must be established and defined by Scripture. The two primary offices within the church are elders and deacons. However, before discussing the particulars of what our elders and deacons should be and do, let us first consider the Chief Shepherd, Jesus Christ.

Chapter 7

THE CHIEF SHEPHERD

Every local church emerges in the world through a team of committed believers. And local churches are led by pastors, who often wear the title of "Senior" or "Lead." Yet we must understand that the existence, stability, growth, and victory of the church is in the sovereign hands of Jesus Christ.

THE FOUNDER OF THE CHURCH

The church exists because Jesus Christ Himself has established it. When one of the disciples confessed Jesus as "the Christ, the Son of the living God" (Matt. 16:16), Jesus responded, "on this rock I will build my church" (Matt. 16:18). Scholars debate what or who the "rock" is. It could be Peter or Peter's confession of Jesus. But what is settled is that Jesus is the one who builds the church. The church is the production of the Savior and is protected by Him. Neither persecution nor hell can tear down what Jesus has built.

Because the blueprint of the church was designed in eternity past, it is not a human invention. It is holy and must be treated as such. A local church should not be operated like a business or run by a board of CEOs. It is neither a country club nor a distributor of religious goods and services. The church is built and led by Jesus Christ as the in-breaking of the kingdom of God into the world. Yes, it is filled with sinners, and the church is imperfect at this stage of redemption. But it remains the holy bride of Christ. This demands that our approach to worship and mission, to all of church life, be characterized by sober and biblical principles.

THE FOUNDATION OF THE CHURCH

Jesus is not only the builder of the church, but also the foundation upon which it is built. As believers, we are "members of the household of God, built on the foundation of the apostles and prophets, Christ Jesus himself being the cornerstone, in whom the whole structure, being joined together, grows into a holy temple in the Lord. In him you also are being built together into a dwelling place for God by the Spirit" (Eph. 2:19–22).

Many churches today attempt to build their ministry upon the persona and gifts of its preaching pastor. Such a leader becomes the identity of a church. He is the attraction, then becomes the brand, and eventually defines the culture of the local body. It often "works," in the sense that large groups are gathered, organized, and multiplied. But such churches draw our attention away from Jesus. Wherever Christ is not at the center, someone or something else will occupy that space, and that will be what comes to define the congregation.

The theological truth that the church is built upon Christ has tremendous implications for every congregation. To say that Jesus is the foundation means that on Him the entire ecclesiastical structure, with all of its walls, rooms, doors, and windows, is continually built. The church expands as more are converted and then discipled. If the foundation is stable, the structure is secure.

Churches come to the end of their life for a variety of reasons, but often it is connected to what the church itself has been built on. Does the church rest upon programs, money, personality, tribalism, or shared affinity? Such foundations are themselves unsteady and will shift with the ground underneath and around them. But if Jesus is the foundation of a church, the church will be stable and safe.

In one sense, Jesus is in fact the foundation of *His* church. And that reality cannot be changed. But in another sense, we must ensure that Jesus is the foundation of our *local* churches. Every local church must build its theology and practice on Christ. And this means that Jesus must be the focus of the local church.

THE FOCUS OF THE CHURCH

You can tell what a church is about by the theology it confesses. Unfortunately, many evangelical churches today do not hold to a historic confession of faith that lays out a clear devotion and robust theology that clarifies its emphasis on Jesus and the gospel. Many rely on a summary "statement of faith" that points to but a few doctrinal points that are held by their leadership.

But even if a church affirms one of the great confessions of faith, it is no guarantee that such theology has truly gripped the congregation. The theology of a church is most clearly seen in the preaching of the church.

Healthy churches come in all shapes and sizes. Different churches find themselves needing to address differing issues and problems based on their context. And different churches will have differing strengths and weaknesses. But every church must be clearly Christ-centered. Jesus is our greatest hope and boast, our deepest longing and joy, and our most passionate song and message. Jesus is our focus because His gospel is what defines us as Christians, unites us as brothers and sisters, transforms us as sinners-yet-saints, and sends us as God's people on mission. When Jesus is the focus, He is exalted above every other good thing in our lives and triumphs over every bad thing set against us.

THE SHEPHERD OF THE CHURCH

In John 10, Jesus teaches us that He is the "good shepherd" of the church. As the Shepherd of the church, Jesus occupies the position of sovereign caregiver. He saves the sheep from danger, knows them by name, provides for their needs, and leads them safely into open pastures of rest. He tells us,

> I am the good shepherd. The good shepherd lays down his life for the sheep. He who is a hired hand and not a shepherd, who does not own the sheep, sees the wolf coming and leaves the sheep and flees, and the wolf snatches them and scatters them. He flees because he is a hired hand and cares nothing for the sheep. I am the good shepherd. I know my own and my own know me, just as the Father knows me and I know the Father; and I lay down my life for the sheep.
>
> (JOHN 10:11–15)

He Saves Us

A shepherd must protect the sheep from dangerous animals and thieves, and our Lord protects the church from the lion who devours (1 Peter 5:8) and the sin that condemns. The devil seeks to attack and destroy Christians, and only Christ the Shepherd is equipped to defend us while defeating him. As John explains, "The reason the Son of God appeared was to destroy the works of the devil" (1 John 3:8). Yet to destroy the evil one, Jesus had to lay down His life. Only by offering Himself as a sacrifice for sin on the cross could the devil be conquered. In Christ's death, the people of God are freed from Satan's grip, cleansed from sin, justified, and reconciled to God.

Yes, the church has many "under-shepherds," or pastors, but man does not have the power to do what only Jesus has accomplished. We worship and follow Jesus, not clergy. Even our leaders are sinners who must submit to and follow the Shepherd of our souls.

The way of Jesus should compel all pastors in the church today to live humble, sacrificial lives that seek the well-being of their congregations, even if it is costly. A pastor who is not willing to defend, serve, and sacrifice for the people of God is not following the example of our Savior, and may not be following Him at all.

He Knows Us

A shepherd knows his sheep. He knows not only that they are sheep, and that they are his responsibility, but he knows them individually. He knows which are stubborn and which are needy. He can call them by name and each one responds to his voice. So it is with Jesus, our Great Shepherd. He knows us by name and knows us well (John 10:3).

When Jesus says that He knows His own, He means more than that He has observed us and knows our habits and tendencies. He means that He knows us deeply, relationally, and that He loves us. He knows our needs and desires, our afflictions and temptations, what we can and cannot handle, and how to best bring us home.

The knowledge that Jesus has of His people is a knowledge that has no beginning and extends into eternity. And it is a knowledge that He does not have of those who are not His own. This does not mean Jesus does not have all knowledge, but that the special knowledge He has of His people is different than His knowledge of those outside the church. Consider what Jesus says to those who do not believe and must stand before Him at the judgment:

> Not everyone who says to me, "Lord, Lord," will enter the kingdom of heaven, but the one who does the will of my Father who is in heaven. On that day many will say to me, "Lord, Lord, did we not prophesy in your name, and cast out demons in your name, and do many mighty works in your name?"

> *And then will I declare to them, "I never knew you;*
> *depart from me, you workers of lawlessness."*
>
> (MATT. 7:21–23; *emphasis added*)

Our Shepherd knows us well, and He is best equipped to lead us. The same must be true of pastors of local churches. It is not enough for elders to simply make decisions or even teach publicly. They must *know* the congregation, collectively and individually. If they do not know their people, they cannot effectively lead or serve them.

He Leads Us

A shepherd leads his sheep out of danger and into pastures where they are able to feed. So Jesus leads His people. But He leads us not only out of danger, but also into victory (2 Cor. 2:14). For He has conquered our enemies and now leads us to spread the news of His victory and our security in Him.

Pastors, therefore, should lead their people well, not only in doctrinal precision, but also in faith, godliness, good works, and true worship. Shepherds do not merely make suggestions and offer alternatives in these areas; they show the way by walking before the people in an example worth following.

—

Chapter 8

ELDERS

A local church is led by a plurality of elders who are committed to the ministry of the Word and prayer. The terms *elder* and *pastor* can be used interchangeably and signify the same office of church leadership. Such men are to be set apart by the congregation, having met the qualifications of elders in 1 Timothy 3. These leaders work together in leading the charge of making and caring for disciples.

QUALIFIED

The qualifications for elders in a local church are laid out in 1 Timothy 3:1–7:

> *The saying is trustworthy: If anyone aspires to the office of overseer, he desires a noble task. Therefore an overseer must be above reproach, the husband of one wife, sober-minded, self-controlled, respectable, hospitable, able to teach, not a drunkard, not violent but gentle, not*

quarrelsome, not a lover of money. He must manage his own household well, with all dignity keeping his children submissive, for if someone does not know how to manage his own household, how will he care for God's church? He must not be a recent convert, or he may become puffed up with conceit and fall into the condemnation of the devil. Moreover, he must be well thought of by outsiders, so that he may not fall into disgrace, into a snare of the devil.

He must be above reproach. This does not mean that an elder must be without sin. If that were the case, then no man could serve as a pastor. In fact, the apostle John says that those who claim to be without sin do not know the truth (1 John 1:5–10). To be above reproach is to live a life of godliness that is visible to others. Not only are the fruits of the Spirit (Gal. 5:22–23) and the following qualifications evident in their lives, but when they sin, they confess and repent openly.

He must be the husband of one wife. While marriage itself is not a prerequisite for a man to serve as an elder, a married elder must be devoted to his wife in his heart and life. Such devotion indicates that he is faithful to his wife and that his marriage is flourishing as a result. He sees the spiritual health of his wife as his first ministry and seeks both her holiness and happiness through a life of self-sacrifice.

He must be sober-minded. Leading others spiritually

requires one to be clear-headed and thoughtful in all serious matters. This means that his priorities are established, his goals have been clarified, and his singularity of thought in ministry leaves little room for confusion over where he is leading his flock.

He must be self-controlled. Elders are to be disciplined and trustworthy. They do not act rashly or impulsively, but have learned patience and live lives characterized by order.

He must be respectable. Another mark of a pastor is his respectable life. This does not mean he has affluence or a high status in society, but that he is stable in character. He is not perceived to be crass or creepy, but is known as a man of charity and grace.

He must be hospitable. Elders have learned from Jesus Christ what it means to welcome strangers and to include outsiders as insiders, sharing his life and gifts with those in need.

He must be able to teach. Because the ministry of the Word is central to the calling of a pastor, he must be apt to teach the truths of Scripture in a way that is comprehensible to the body of Christ. This does not require all elders to be competent in public preaching. Rather, they must be able to handle rightly the Word of God.

He must not be a drunkard. While alcohol consumption itself is not forbidden, drunkenness is. And the prohibition against intoxication goes beyond the abuse of alcohol and includes the misuse and abuse of all created things. Because the danger of drunkenness and gluttony is real—and often not observable by others—leaders must follow Paul's advice to live carefully in our dangerous and fallen world (Eph. 5:15–16).

He must be gentle. Unrighteous anger and rage are not only unbecoming for a leader, but also show him to be ill-suited for serving sinful people. Ministering to people in the midst of their temptations and failures requires incredible patience.

He must not be quarrelsome. The command to avoid fighting is a call to live peacefully. To be sure, an elder must be ready to contend for the faith, even to "fight the good fight of the faith" (1 Tim. 6:12), but he must not be needlessly quarrelsome. Leaders who looks for fights are sure to find them, and such action typically distracts them from the mission Christ gave the church.

He must not be a lover of money. Most pastors do not receive generous salaries serving a local church. But this does not mean the love of money is not a real struggle for them. The heart is easily captivated by worldly treasures, and leaders who love money are prone to discontentment and poor stewardship of God's resources.

He must shepherd his home. If a pastor cannot lead his home, then he cannot lead a church. Of course, he may be effective at leading a congregation while neglecting his family. But such reveals the idolization of ministry and the refusal to care for the most important people under his care. Integral to shepherding his home is active love and service of his family. As a result, his children respect and respond positively to his leadership. This does not mean a pastor's children are always a model for others. They are sinners, and will, at times, rebel. Such corruption in the children of church leaders does not disqualify them from leading. But how they handle their children when they rebel is critical in demonstrating how well they care for their household.

He must be a mature believer. The caveat that an elder must not be a recent convert means that he must be a mature believer. This is not necessarily an indication of age, but of time spent following Jesus. His faith must be stable. An immature leader is likely to become either prideful of his quickly acquired status or fearful of his new and often overwhelming responsibilities.

He must have a good reputation. Even the reputation of an elder outside of the church matters. He can be publicly hated for righteousness' sake, but he should not be thought of as an untrustworthy, unstable, or immoral man.

These are the moral and spiritual qualities expected of an elder. While no Christian is perfect, and a godly leader may be stronger or weaker in any of these qualities, an elder will exhibit both the presence and growth of these virtues.

CALLED

Even if a man meets the qualifications of an elder, he may not desire to serve as an elder. In fact, he may not even be called to serve as an elder. The issue of "calling" has fallen out of favor in the minds of many today, but it is an important aspect of one's suitability for leading in the local church.

Before a church calls a qualified man to serve as an elder, God has already called him, or set him apart for the task. How does one determine whether he is called to serve in such a capacity? He must have a desire to serve as pastor and demonstrate fruitfulness in the work of ministry, and the local church must confirm the call he feels inwardly. These three elements work together to identify the one who is called.

Desire

Those who will serve as an elder will desire to do the work. They will, as Paul says to Timothy, "aspire" to the office (1 Tim 3:1). This desire may be a long-standing desire, or it may develop quickly as he is discipled, mentored, and helped to see his particular set of gifts. But eventually, he will be burdened with a desire to preach Christ, warning and teaching all people in wisdom with the aim of seeing them grow into mature disciples of our Lord (Col. 1:28–29).

Fruitfulness

Desire alone, however, is not enough to determine whether one is called. The call of God to pastoral ministry, or any ministry for that matter, will produce fruit in the work accomplished. The fruit born in the life of one who is called is seen in how the church receives his instruction, follows his lead, and is impacted by his ministry even before he is appointed to an official position.

Affirmation

The final piece of the puzzle that clarifies whether one is call to pastoral ministry is the confirmation of his desire by the local church. No church needs or benefits from self-appointed leaders. But churches will recognize those in whom the Spirit of God is at work to serve the body in this particular way.

Shepherds

Pastors are not corporate businessmen running a non profit organization. They are not mere decision makers. They are, fundamentally, *shepherds*, as the word *pastor* comes from the Latin word meaning "shepherd."

As we discussed earlier, shepherding is not about managing an organization, but about leading and serving a people. It demands that leaders know the congregation, and that the congregation knows its leaders. It requires transparency and trust from both sides of the pulpit and the counseling chair. Shepherding demands elders to be up close and hands-on in the lives of those under their care.

Shepherds do not spend all their time in the study, but are regularly with their people in both formal and informal capacities. Of course, shepherding well demands an elder to be devoted to prayer and the study of God's Word. But what is cultivated in times of solitude must be worked out in preaching, teaching, weddings, funerals, counseling, visitation, hanging out, recreation, and more.

THEOLOGIANS

An elder is nothing if he is not a theologian. Theology is often said to be the study of the God, but I think a better way to explain theology is to say that it is the understanding and communication of the knowledge of God. The term *theology* itself literally means "a word about God." So the task of the theologian is not merely *comprehending* the truth of God, but also *communicating* the truth of God.

Theologians speak. They write. They warn of God's judgment and encourage with God's promises. They make plain the wonders of the Almighty. There is nothing to preach without theology, nor is there any lasting counsel apart from doctrine. Theology gives the church a true, if incomplete, picture of God and humanity.

And it is the task of the pastor-theologian to defend the church against the dangers of heresy and false doctrine that has led many away from the truth and away from the church.

Ultimately, the church is called to worship our triune God, and worship is simply impossible apart from theology. As many like to say, the goal of theology (the knowledge of God) is doxology (the praise of God).

Chapter 9

DEACONS

The church is served by deacons appointed to manage various ministry responsibilities and to attend needs felt across a diverse body. The first deacons were appointed to address an immediate need in the early church related to the neglect of the Greek-speaking widows (Acts 6:1–6).

The difference between deacons and elders is that of both function and authority. Deacons are tasked with important ministry responsibilities that would interfere with elders' primary responsibilities of the ministry of the Word and prayer (Acts 6:2). Deacons serve the needs and interests of the local church under the authority and oversight of the elders. They are depicted as having authority in or oversight of the church as elders are, but are set apart by the church and governed by the elders.

The need for deacons is just as critical today as it was in the first century. As our churches experience numerical growth and become more diverse, different needs arise that are within the church's responsibility to address.

Deacons are, in some sense, first responders. They identify problems, develop solutions, and work with the elders to ensure that the entire body is being cared for. From the management of particular systems to the training of volunteers for specific work to the distribution of benevolence funds, deacons are critical for maintaining a healthy church.

The church cannot function properly without elders or deacons. Both offices have a divine origin, and those who serve in these roles must be qualified and called.

Like those for elders, the qualifications for deacons are seen in 1 Timothy 3:

> Deacons likewise must be dignified, not double-tongued, not addicted to much wine, not greedy for dishonest gain. They must hold the mystery of the faith with a clear conscience. And let them also be tested first; then let them serve as deacons if they prove themselves blameless. Their wives likewise must be dignified, not slanderers, but sober-minded, faithful in all things. Let deacons each be the husband of one wife, managing their children and their own households well. For those who serve well as deacons gain a good standing for themselves and also great confidence in the faith that is in Christ Jesus.
>
> (VV. 8–13)

Deacons must be "dignified," meaning that they are worthy of respect with godly character that is evident to all. The requirement of self-control—included in the list of qualifications for elders—is emphasized here in not being "double-tongued."

Along with elders, they cannot be addicted to or captivated by alcohol. They also must be content with their station in life, not greedy or materialistic.

Deacons hold the mystery of the faith with a clear conscience. Therefore, they must possess a clear understanding of the gospel and a faith that is active in producing good works.

Just as elders must not be recent converts, so deacons must be "tested" before they are appointed to their office. The testing that Paul mentions does not mean that deacons must pass a formal test for ministry, but that they have been proven in character in their time in the local church.

While the office of elder is limited to qualified and called men, the diaconate is made up of men and women who are qualified and called. Paul, in the midst of discussing the qualifications of deacons, begins to discuss women. The English Standard Version translates this Greek word as "wives," but it can also be translated "women." That Paul is likely not addressing the wives of deacons but women who serve as deacons is seen in that he does not mention the elders' wives in the preceding passage pertaining to elders. Paul says that women serving the church in this role must also be "dignified," controlled with their words, sober-minded, and faithful in all things.

The local church needs women serving as deacons: first, because it is biblical (Rom. 16:1–2) and, second, because without both men and women serving in this role, the body is likely to be less cared for and less protected. Women often have different needs than men and benefit from other, mature Christian women serving them. Deacons address a broader range of ministry needs than the elders do, and without godly women serving in such a role, the church is ill-equipped to care for her members.

Only when a congregation has a plurality of both deacons and elders leading and serving together can a church thrive in its mission to make disciples.

—

Chapter 10

THE CONGREGATION

Many churches today treat church members, if they even have formal membership, as mere spectators. The Bible, however, teaches that we are a body of congregants, not consumers. Members are participants, not patrons. The church is not simply a religious organization, but a family that exists in covenant together.

MEMBERSHIP

The idea of church membership has fallen on hard times. Many churches forgo the idea of membership, and others have a kind of "spiritual membership" but no actual membership. This typically means that the people have no accountability to the larger body. Some object to membership on the grounds that it is not biblical, while others object to it as an impracticality or a hindrance to church growth.

That church membership is a biblical concept is seen in that local churches knew exactly who was a part of the church. As men and women accepted the gospel and were baptized, they were "added" to the local church (Acts 2:41, 47; 5:14; 16:5). Pastors are tasked with leading, teaching, overseeing, and shepherding the people of the church (Heb. 13:17; 1 Tim. 5:17). Such a task is nearly impossible without having a way to know who is and is not part of the church.

Moreover, unless there is a kind of membership in which Christians are bound together in local churches, the responsibility of exercising church discipline becomes more complicated. How can someone in the church be corrected, restored, or excommunicated if there is not a formal means of tracking who is part of the local body?

Church membership is not like membership in a local country club or gym. It is more like membership in a family. But even this analogy falls short. Membership in the church is based on our union with Christ and is demonstrated through a voluntary, formal commitment to one another in a local context. Membership is a way in which we live in covenant for the glory of God and the good of the church. It is a promise to partner with one another in carrying out the Great Commission and a willingness to hold one another accountable in our journeys of faith.

Church membership determines who is and is not "in" the church, and then determines who will play a role in the direction and work of the church. Members of the church I serve have the responsibility of appointing leaders, receiving and removing members, and affirming a budget on which the church will operate. Without membership, such responsibilities would fall entirely into the hands of just a few leaders, which would be overwhelming and would probably distract them from other responsibilities with which they have been entrusted.

UNITY AND DIVERSITY

A congregation, if healthy, will be diverse yet unified. Diversity has become a popular idea for many churches today, though many remain confused about what it should look like or how it can be achieved. Truthfully, diversity will look different in each city, community, and neighborhood. One church may have a geographical reach that includes a variety of ethnicities and cultures, while another may find itself in an area characterized entirely by one group of people yet be diverse in other ways. Regardless of the context, diversity remains possible and should be the natural consequence of evangelism, discipleship, and hospitality as lived out in the life of a church.

The diversity of a local church should reflect the diversity of its context. A church in a city with one ethnicity making up over 90 percent of the population should still reflect diversity in at least proportionate measure. Perhaps the church will have around 90 percent of the people sharing that same skin color, but diversity should also be seen generationally, socioeconomically, and subculturally.

Because the kingdom of God is made up of people from every tribe, tongue, and nation, purchased by Jesus Christ in His death on the cross, our churches should reflect the power of the gospel and the diversity of the kingdom as much as is possible.

While there must be unity in our diversity, it is not our diversity that unifies us any more than homogeneity unifies. The unity of the church is not found in shared affinities, but in a common faith in a shared Savior.

ACCOUNTABILITY

Accounts of church leaders falling into grievous sin, abusing their power, and leading churches into ruin seem all too common today. Many church members have found themselves not only in the dark about what their leadership is doing, but also without recourse when leaders drift away from sound doctrine or pious living. A healthy church has not only a plurality of elders who lead well, but also a congregation that holds one another, including its leadership, accountable.

Yes, many churches have been undone by congregations. Congregationalism—a system of church governance in which the local congregation is independent of others and directs its own affairs—often gets a bad name, and it is often well warranted. Churches that are micromanaged by the opinions of cliques in the pews show a lack of unity and focus on the mission Christ gave the church. Churches have been destroyed by elder rule, congregational rule, and every form of church government in between. And until Jesus returns, the church will continue to struggle to get church governance right. Nevertheless, every church needs cooperative accountability between pastors and the congregation.

Elders are established by God to govern, oversee, and exercise authority in the church. But who holds them accountable? What role does the membership of the church play in the church's decision making? Scripture gives us two explicit roles and one implicit.

Church Discipline

That the congregation is involved in church discipline—which we will discuss in detail in part 4—is clear in both Matthew 18 and 1 Corinthians 5. The pattern and progression of church discipline, if necessary, is: first, patient and private accountability and guidance, then toward public warning, and finally removal from membership by the congregation as a whole. Jesus said,

> *If your brother sins against you, go and tell him his fault, between you and him alone. If he listens to you, you have gained your brother. But if he does not listen, take one or two others along with you, that every charge may be established by the evidence of two or three witnesses. If he refuses to listen to them, tell it to the church. And if he refuses to listen even to the church, let him be to you as a Gentile and a tax collector. Truly, I say to you, whatever you bind on earth shall be bound in heaven, and whatever you loose on earth shall be loosed in heaven. Again I say to you, if two of you agree on earth about anything they ask, it will be done for them by my Father in heaven. For where two or three are gathered in my name, there am I among them.*
>
> (MATT. 18:15–20)

The congregation must get involved in the matter of church discipline when a member, including a leader, has continued in unrepentant sin. The church must be told of his or her impenitence. If they remain unmoved by the prayers and loving correction of the congregation, the individual must then be removed from membership by the church collectively (1 Cor. 5:9–13)

It is not just to elders that members are held accountable, but to the church as a whole. A church that is not a part of the process of discipline cannot be healthy or effective in caring for the people.

Appointing Leadership

Establishing leadership in the local church also appears to be a cooperative effort between elders and congregants. While Scripture does not provide detailed procedures for establishing elders and deacons in the church, what is clear is congressional involvement and accountability. We see both elders and congregations involved in the appointment of leadership (Acts 6:3; 14:23). While elders should seek out and train people to serve and lead in the church, the congregation must participate in the process by confirming who will be appointed to lead.

Financial Accountability

Scripture makes clear that local churches should take up a collection for the needs of ministry (1 Cor. 16:1). What is not clear, however, is who determines how the money is spent. It is wise for the elders to be as transparent as possible in constructing a budget that the congregation will vote to affirm. A lack of transparency concerning the money collected can breed distrust and inhibits accountability.

PART 4

DISCIPLINE PRACTICED *with* GRACE

hurch discipline takes two forms: formative and reformative. Formative discipline is the regular, ongoing work of positive discipleship that comes through preaching, teaching, mentoring, friendship, service, and worship. Reformative discipline is corrective discipline that addresses serious sin in the lives of church members and aims at ultimately leading them away from sin and closer to Jesus. Spousal or child abuse, drunkenness, sexual immorality, and gossip are just some of the serious sins that have brought ruin to the lives of people and thus warrant corrective restorative discipline. The goal of both forms of discipline is fostering a vibrant and mature faith in the people. However, when most people speak of church discipline, they are generally referring to reformative discipline.

Reformative church discipline is rarely practiced today. Even among those who do practice it, we see many examples of church discipline gone wrong. Church discipline must be taken seriously by the whole church and conducted in a spirit of love and grace.

In chapter 10, we discussed briefly Matthew 18, a key passage that informs the practice of church reformative discipline. Yet in this part, we will explore the passage further. Here, Jesus gives us a model to follow in helping a brother or sister who has sinned against another, and what to do if they remain impenitent.

To many, what Jesus prescribes seems like an invasion of privacy. And because some churches that do practice reformative discipline have unfortunately abused their members during the discipline process, some churches avoid such abuses by eliminating reformative discipline altogether. But church discipline is a necessary aspect of church life and health, and should therefore be approached with care and practiced with grace.

Church discipline is the means by which members trapped in serious sin can receive specific, targeted help and accountability. It is also the means by which other members in the church are protected from the harmful effects of others' sin. A church that practices church discipline well is a church that demonstrates real care for the entire body through accountability, correction, instruction, and ultimately restoration.

Chapter 11

GO TO YOUR BROTHER

The first step in reestablishing the fellowship that has been broken between two Christians is to address the issue privately. Jesus says, "If your brother sins against you, go and tell him his fault, between you and him alone. If he listens to you, you have gained your brother." (Matt. 18:15). What Jesus prescribes here is supposed to be a normal aspect of the Christian life. When such action is necessary, it is the responsibility of every Christian to initiate reconciliation. We are not to wait for the other person to make the first step.

When Christians are in the midst of conflict, there are only two appropriate responses to the situation: repentance and forgiveness. If you are confronting one who has sinned against you, your desire should be reconciliation and your duty is to forgive. We are tempted to hold grudges or to seek retribution. But as Christ has forgiven us, so we must forgive one another (Col. 3:13). And if you are the one being approached for wronging, you must be quick to listen and slow to speak. And when you do speak, you should confess your sin and ask for forgiveness.

Most of the relational drama that creeps into churches would be settled quickly if Christians would simply follow Jesus' counsel in Matthew 18.

Regarding formal church discipline, elders should come alongside a member caught in sin only on account of serious and sustained transgression. Every Christian sins and fails, and these common experiences are not cause for the sober work of restoration. But grievous sin, or prolonged impenitence, is the ground for initiating discipline.

This requires compassion and wisdom since Scripture does not provide a list to determine what is and is not worthy of church discipline. However, sin that is dangerous to one's, or someone else's, physical or spiritual health warrants investigation and counsel. Church discipline is not the only appropriate response to every sinful behavior. If someone in the church is physically abusive, or engaging in other illegal activities, the leadership has the responsibility to notify the police.

Approaching an individual who may need to come under discipline should be done sensitively. Elders should come alongside a brother or sister in order to investigate what condition they are in and to offer practical help. If church leaders have truly shepherded their people, then members are more likely to be open about their sin and receptive to pastoral care. Ultimately, discipline *is* pastoral care. This is much more than pointing out sin. It is mentoring, modeling, and instructing. It includes the constant investment of the gospel into the lives of those caught in sin and therefore at spiritual risk. Discipline also includes helpful strategies to leverage means of grace as they begin to draw near to the Lord.

The purpose of church discipline is not punitive, but restorative. It is not to punish, but to rescue sinners from harm. In every stage of discipline, from beginning to end, the goal is to bring back a sinner from his wandering and save his soul from death (James 5:20).

EXPAND CARE WHILE
EXPRESSING CONCERN

If a church member who is in serious sin remains resistant to repentance or hostile to help, Jesus calls us to return to them again and "take one or two others along with you, that every charge may be established by the evidence of two or three witnesses" (Matt. 18:16). This serves two purposes. The first is to clarify the severity and danger of their sin and to testify the hope of the gospel. The second is to show just how loved the individual is. We are called to offer help and hope, to point them to Jesus, who stands ready to receive all who come to Him poor in spirit. One's impenitence does not change the ultimate aim of discipline, which is restoration.

In the context of church discipline, an elder should return to the wayward individual with another elder or with someone else capable in assisting. Practicing church discipline with grace and truth requires patience. The individual may not respond repentantly right away. Oftentimes, the elders will need to allow time for the individual to become receptive to Scripture and the work of the Holy Spirit. It may take days, weeks, or even longer for the individual to respond to the Spirit's conviction. It would be wise, therefore, for the elders to visit the person multiple times before taking the matter to the entire congregation.

What church discipline looks like at this stage varies from case to case. In some situations, all that is needed is accountability and assistance, while others may need to step down from serving or leading in the church. Those refusing to repent are temporarily excluded from the Lord's Supper until they demonstrate godly sorrow and a hatred for their sin (2 Cor. 7:9–11).

If the individual responds in repentance and trust in the gospel, then discipline may pause at this stage as the brother or sister begins to make progress. Just as sanctification is a process that takes time, so church discipline often takes time as those under the care of the elders relearn to seek the Lord. Even though discipline may come to an end, the individual may need continuing counsel and encouragement as they move forward in their faith journey. And in such cases, the whole matter of their discipline has remained a private affair.

Chapter 12

TELL IT TO THE CHURCH

If the person refuses to listen to the patient appeals of the elders and continues in sin, the issue needs to be brought before the church (Matt. 18:17). The reason that a member's private business needs to become somewhat public, at least in terms of sharing this with the church family of which he belongs, is because his impenitence is likely to cause harm to himself and others, and even damage the reputation of Christ's church.

In a day when people value privacy, want to mind their own business, and want others to stay out of their business, this stage of restorative discipline seems absurd. Despite the spirit of our day, Jesus calls us to take such matters to the church, for we are not dealing with a lone individual, but a member of God's family for whom the entire local church is responsible.

Again, the aim here is the same as before: to see the

member restored to faith and godliness; to shape them, not shame them. This stage of discipline should be done in a setting where the church family can talk through the issue and pray for the wayward member. It should be a time of grieving and seeking God's intervention.

Bringing the situation before the church contributes in several ways to hopefully restoring the individual. It can bring sobering pressure upon the wandering member. He knows that his church family now knows his sin. As a result, he will no longer be able to pretend that everything in his life is okay. Because his situation has become public, he will be faced in a more serious way with the call to deal with his sin. This stage of discipline allows for the member to reflect on his life, the condition of his soul, the height from which he has fallen, and the need for him to repent (Rev. 2:5).

Bringing the matter before the church also means that more people will pray for and potentially reach out to their brother or sister in danger. Hope is not lost. The church is in fact closer to seeing a work of God accomplished in bringing about restoration.

Most of us heard the warnings of judgment and the hope of the gospel several times before we repented of our sin and trusted in Jesus. And much of our spiritual growth is a slow process of hearing and obeying God's Word. The elders and the church must be reasonably patient in dealing with someone under this stage in discipline as restoration is pursued.

REMOVAL FROM MEMBERSHIP

If the person under discipline continues in sin after the elders and the church have pursued restoring him, patiently and prayerfully seeking his good, he must be removed from membership (Matt. 18:17).

This course of action is not to be applied to those under discipline who are diligently seeking restoration but are still struggling or even failing. Without any repentance, however, there is no other recourse for the body of Christ than to remove the individual from the fellowship. The church cannot condone sin. Nor can it give false assurance of one's spiritual health. The individual has not repented and has not shown a desire to change. Trust in the gospel, therefore, is not evident in his life.

Such a person is not merely released from membership, but is excommunicated, meaning that he is no longer recognized as a Christian. His continuation in serious sin and claim to be a Christian is a dangerous form of hypocrisy that warrants separation. Paul wrote,

> *I wrote to you in my letter not to associate with sexually immoral people—not at all meaning the sexually immoral of this world, or the greedy and*

> swindlers, or idolaters, since then you would need
> to go out of the world. But now I am writing to you
> not to associate with anyone who bears the name of
> brother if he is guilty of sexual immorality or greed,
> or is an idolater, reviler, drunkard, or swindler—
> not even to eat with such a one.

(1 COR. 5:9–13)

What Paul is prescribing is separation, not shunning. The call is to abstain from fellowshiping with such a person as if he or she were still a part of the church family. This does not mean, however, that members of the church cannot contact, spend time with, or show love and kindness to the person. The church has not given up on him. This is the final stage of church discipline, which has the same aim of restoration. So even though drastic measures are taken, they are taken in hopes that he will someday submit his life to Christ. And until then, it is indeed good for members of the church to demonstrate the lovingkindness of Christ to him, just as they would to any unbeliever.

In many cases, the one removed from membership is not barred from attending worship gatherings. Rather, he is encouraged to come and hear the Word preached. But he is no longer welcomed at the Lord's Supper, since the prerequisite for partaking in the meal is faith and repentance. The distance he has created between himself, the church, and the Lord is a loss that he must feel if he is to be restored. Even in this state—especially in this state—the hope is that the gospel of God will awaken him so that he will become sensitive to his sin and his need for grace.

A healthy church will practice discipline in truth and grace, for the good of the people and the glory of God among His people. It is a powerful means by which people are helped and restored in the midst of dangerous sin.

PART 5

the MISSION SHARED BY ALL

Today, confusion abounds concerning the mission of the church. Judging by the "mission statements" of many local churches and some of the popular books being written today, it is apparent that some believe the mission of the church is to improve our cities and our neighbors' quality of life. These are good endeavors that should be organically connected to the life of the church, to be sure. But this is not our mission.

The confusion often comes when we conflate two different responsibilities given to the church. One responsibility is called the Great Commission (Matt. 28:18–20), and the other the Great Commandment (Matt. 22:37–40).

The Great Commission is the central task of the church and can be accomplished only by the church. Our mission, and therefore our primary responsibility, is to make disciples.

Jesus calls the church to preach the gospel and teach the Scripture in such a way that people are converted and then matured in the faith. Conversion is not the mission. Indoctrination is not the mission. The mission is to make disciples. Conversion marks the beginning of discipleship, and instruction and teaching are means of discipleship. But disciples are made in the context of community, where our doctrine and teaching are put into the realities of everyday life through mentoring and peer-to-peer gospel relationships.

The Great Commission is about making disciples, not renewing cities. Historically the church has not had much success in, or focus on, city renewal. The historical church has appropriately focused on changing lives and renewing hearts through the means of grace. As Paul said, we proclaim Jesus Christ, "warning everyone and teaching everyone with all wisdom, that we may present everyone mature in Christ" (Col. 1:28–29). Cities tend to work against the very values and efforts of the church. This does not mean that the church gives up on the city. But it is the Great Commission—making disciples—and not city renewal that moves the church to love our neighbors and seek their well-being.

The Great Commandment is the call to love God and neighbor, to do good to those outside of the church, regardless of their faith or morality. The church bears the responsibility to feed the hungry and clothe the naked, and this is carried out by disciples who follow Jesus. But note the distinction. The mission of the church is to make disciples, and as disciples we love and serve those around us. This is not likely to change the entire city. That is not our goal anyway. Our goal is to see God change lives, to raise the spiritual dead to new life in Jesus Christ. This is the transformation with which we are ultimately concerned.

Chapter 13

EVANGELISM

The mission of the church cannot take place apart from evangelism. Evangelism is the verbal communication of the gospel of Jesus Christ with the aim of seeing people believe in Him and begin a life of following Him. Conversion is the starting point of discipleship, and evangelism aims to convert. The church seeks to convert unbelievers, not through coercion or manipulation, but by proclaiming the truth of Jesus' life, death, and resurrection. And such proclamation is the responsibility of the church at large. It is not only the calling of clergy, but the duty of all disciples.

The New Testament teaches that all Christians are called to bear witness to Christ. Yet the act of witnessing will look different for everyone, often depending on ability, opportunity, and context. Some will share the gospel almost daily, while others will have fewer occasions. But all of us are called to confess Christ publicly (Matt. 10:32–33).

The apostle Peter emphasizes the need to take the opportunities given to us to testify to our faith and the Lordship of Christ. He says, "In your hearts honor Christ the Lord as holy, always being prepared to make a defense to anyone who asks you for a reason for the hope that is in you; yet do it with gentleness and respect" (1 Peter 3:15).

Evangelism should happen in our homes with our children, in our relationships outside of the church, and as far as our influence will permit. Some Christians are wired in such a way that evangelism will most naturally happen in the context of trusted friendships, while others are called to engage strangers with the gospel. But all Christians are called ambassadors, having been entrusted with the ministry of reconciliation in which we seek to reconcile sinners to our Holy God through Jesus Christ:

> Therefore, if anyone is in Christ, he is a new creation. The old has passed away; behold, the new has come. All this is from God, who through Christ reconciled us to himself and gave us the ministry of reconciliation; that is, in Christ God was reconciling the world to himself, not counting their trespasses against them, and entrusting to us the message of reconciliation. Therefore, we are ambassadors for Christ, God making his appeal through us. We implore you on behalf of Christ, be reconciled to

*God. For our sake he made him to be sin who knew
no sin, so that in him we might become the righteousness of God.*

(2 COR. 5:17–21)

God wants us, people who have been born again by
the power of the Holy Spirit and reconciled to God, to
share our faith so that others may come to know the joy
we possess in the God worth knowing. God uses the
church, all of us, to make His appeal to the world: that
those far from the Lord would draw near, confessing
Jesus Christ as Lord, who is risen from the dead.

While many believers view evangelism as the work
of pastors and not of the entire church, few pastors actu-
ally preach the gospel outside of the gathered church on
the Lord's Day. Of course, the gospel must be preached
on the Lord's Day, both to those who believe as well as
to those among us who do not. But ministers are called
to do more than preach the gospel in their Sunday sermons. They are called to "do the work of an evangelist"
(2 Tim. 4:5).

It is easy for pastors to become so busy with ministering to their congregations that they hardly have relationships with people outside the church. But the work
of an evangelist will take him outside the community
of faith and into the world to share the promise of the
forgiveness of sins and the hope of eternal life.

For a church to be characterized with an evangelistic spirit, the leadership must model the discipline of evangelism. Elders and their message should be known in the community. They should seek to cultivate relationships with their neighbors in which they love and serve them well. And Christian love will seek not only someone's temporal good, but ultimately their eternal good.

Churches who take the mission of the church seriously will approach evangelism strategically. They will plan for it, train for it, and prepare for it—from informal testimony to formal gatherings to creative means by which the gospel is made clear to everyone who can hear it.

Sadly, some Christians are so worried about or critical of evangelizing the wrong way that they never get around to doing it at all. Evangelistic churches will take risks. They would rather try and fail than not try at all.

For the church to make disciples, we must evangelize. We must be present in the surrounding community and prepared to tell the truth of our Savior who lived, died, rose, and lives forevermore.

Chapter 14

DISCIPLESHIP

Making disciples requires a practical, intentional process by which believers are made mature in the faith. Local churches are free to develop rhythms of systems that will best serve their people in discipleship, but there are three necessary aspects to discipleship that no church can afford to neglect and that no Christian can choose to not participate in.

CORPORATE WORSHIP

Corporate worship on the Lord's Day is one of the primary means by which disciples are made. In this gathering, the Word of God is read and preached. The church is taught by the pastors, and members gain an understanding of who God is, how He has worked in our world, and what He has revealed to us. In this gathering, we learn how to interpret Scripture and apply it to our lives.

When the church is gathered together, we also pray

prayers of confession, adoration, and petition. The children of God learn not only various kinds of prayers, but the language of prayer as well. As the church prays, and God answers, the whole congregation sees and can testify to God's work among them.

Music has been lost to performance and pop culture. Most Americans do not sing together as a habit, but here the church stands in a different tradition. We do not gather to watch professionals perform, but to sing ourselves to the God who listens. In singing, we exalt and are exulting in our triune God. Song reinforces in our hearts and minds that God desires our affections, not simply our actions.

Corporate worship also serves in making disciples by bringing together the community of faith. On the Lord's Day, we see God's people, a diverse body of believers united in Christ, confessing one faith and one Lord.

Worship extends beyond the gathering into every facet of life, but it is corporate worship that orients the entire life of a disciple. Our gathering with the church corrects the encroaching false impressions of the world about God through the preaching of the Word, calls us to repent of sin and trust in Jesus, and sends us back out into the world to live, work, and play as the redeemed community of our risen Savior.

RELATIONAL EDIFICATION

As important as corporate worship is, Christians simply cannot do or be what God has called us to do and be apart from relational edification. Intimate, gospel-centered relationships are critical to the task of discipleship because this is the context in which the church fulfills the "one another" commands in Scripture. Only in relationships can we:

- "be at peace with one another" (Mark 9:50)
- "love one another with brotherly affection" (Rom. 12:10)
- "outdo one another in showing honor" (Rom. 12:10)
- "live in harmony with one another" (Rom. 12:16)
- "not pass judgment on one another" (Rom. 14:13)
- "welcome one another" (Rom. 15:7)
- "bear one another's burdens" (Gal. 6:2)
- "be patient, bearing with one another in love" (Eph. 4:2)
- "be kind to one another" (Eph. 4:32)
- "[submit] to one another out of reverence for Christ" (Eph. 5:21)
- "teach and admonish one another" (Col. 3:16)
- "stir up one another to love and good works" (Heb. 10:24)

- "[encourage] one another" (Heb. 10:25)
- and "confess [our] sins to one another and pray for one another" (James 5:16)

Friendships built within the church give us the opportunity to practice the faith and grow in faith as we learn from each other (Rom. 1:11–12). This is also the context where one-on-one mentoring and personal rebuke take place. It is also the context in which we can rejoice with those who rejoice and weep with those who weep.

THE PRACTICE OF MINISTRY

That God calls all Christians to ministry and service is clear in Scripture: "For you were called to freedom, brothers. Only do not use your freedom as an opportunity for the flesh, but through love serve one another" (Gal. 5:13)

Elders are responsible for equipping church members to do the work of ministry so that everyone would be built up in the faith (Eph. 4:12). This means that church members should look for both formal and informal opportunities to minister, and the leadership of the church should provide such opportunities. Whether serving as a greeter on Sunday, teaching children in Sunday school, cleaning the sanctuary, or leading a small group, all service done for the good of the body will help the church and its members flourish in the faith.

Service is the method for making disciples: it teaches believers to sacrifice their time and energy in order to bless others. And such joyful self-denial helps to conform us to the image of Christ.

The mission of the church must be shared by all because we want to see all made complete in Christ. Discipleship is a holistic endeavor, targeting the whole church, challenging the entire life of the people, and is accomplished when the church works together.

Again, at the heart of all this—and eveything we have discussed—is the gospel, which gives life to the entire local body. And the character of a church, which is formed by the gospel, establishes its priorities, direction, and strength. Healthy and faithful churches driven by the gospel intentionally maintain the ministry of the Word and the ordinances under the leadership of God-called, church-affirmed elders, practice discipline with grace, and continually embrace the mission to make disciples.

NOTES

Introduction

1. "The Baptist Confession of Faith," 26.1, on *The Voice of the Reformation* website, http://www.vor.org/truth/1689/1689bc00 .html.

Chapter 1: The Bible's Authority

1. "The Baptist Confession of Faith," 1.1, on *The Voice of the Reformation* website, http://www.vor.org/truth/1689/1689bc00.html.
2. Ibid.

Chapter 2: The Bible's Sufficiency

1. As explained in the "Westminster Shorter Catechism," Q. 4, on the Orthodox Presbyterian Church website, http://www.opc .org/sc.html. See also Psalm 90:2; Malachi 3:6; John 4:24.
2. For more on this, see the introduction to my book *Note to Self: The Discipline of Preaching to Yourself* (Wheaton, IL: Crossway, 2011).

Chapter 5: Christ's Body Broken and Blood Spilled

1. "The Baptist Confession of Faith," 30.7, on *The Voice of the Reformation* website, http://www.vor.org/truth/1689/1689bc00.html.
2. Richard Barcellos, *The Lord's Supper as a Means of Grace: More than a Memory* (Fearn, Scotland: Christian Focus Publications, 2013), 52.

3. James P. Boyce, *Abstract of Systematic Theology* (Hanford, CA: Den Dulk Christian Foundation), chapter 37.

4. Barcellos, *The Lord's Supper*, 68.

5. Ray Van Neste, "The Lord's Supper in the Context of the Local Church," in *The Lord's Supper: Remembering and Proclaiming Christ Until He Comes*, ed. Thomas R. Schreiner and Matthew R. Crawford (Nashville: B&H Academic, 2011), 373.

Chapter 6: Fencing the Table

1. John Bunyan, *Differences in Judgment About Water Baptism No Bar to Communion*, The Works of John Bunyan, Vol. 2 (Carlisle, PA: Banner of Truth Trust, 1991), 617.

2. "The Baptist Confession of Faith," 30.1, on *The Voice of the Reformation* website, http://www.vor.org/truth/1689/1689bc00 .html.

ACKNOWLEDGMENTS

I would like to thank Paul Maxwell for encouraging me to write this book and introducing me to Moody Publishers. Thanks to Drew Dyck, acquisitions editor, and Kevin Emmert, developmental editor, for helping me clarify and better communicate what is on my heart. This book is greatly improved by your efforts.

Thanks to the leadership of Redeemer Fellowship—Jeff Willey, Pat Aldridge, Brian Malcolm, Rob Warford, and Jimmy Fowler—and the entire congregation for showing me what a healthy church looks like in real life.

And thank you to my wife, Jen, and our children, Katherine, Elias, Madeline, and Kilian, for being patient with me during the time it took to write this book.

THE life | heart | character OF THE CHURCH

This three-book series is designed for diverse readership. It avoids theological jargon and uses clear terms to keep readers tracking and engaged. Ideal for evangelism and discipleship, each book can be read within an hour and is organized simply for retention. Biblical, balanced, and historically informed, it is useful for Sunday school, one-to-one reading, ministry training, and personal study.

FOR THE
CHURCH

FTC.CO

MOODY
Publishers

moodypublishers.com

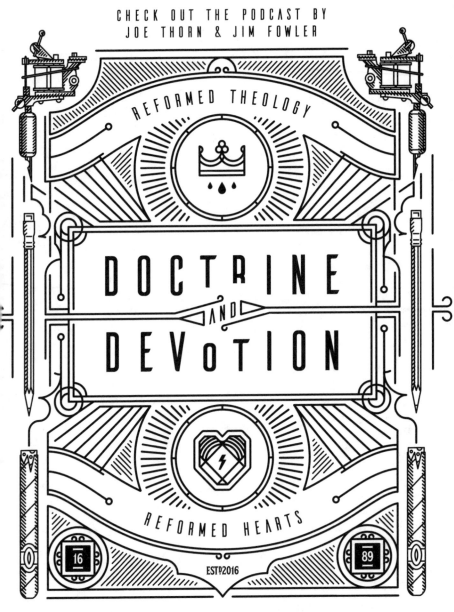

CHECK OUT THE PODCAST BY
JOE THORN & JIM FOWLER

REFORMED THEOLOGY

DOCTRINE
AND
DEVOTION

REFORMED HEARTS

ESTD 2016

WWW.DOCTRINEANDDEVOTION.COM